SKJERVEN GAARD

VIK

SOGN OG FJORDANE

NORWAY:

1669 – 1922

From Church Registers of Baptisms, Deaths, and Marriages in parts of Sogn og Fjordane County.

Compiled by **DONOVAN HURST**

March 24, 2012

Dedication

This work is dedicated to all of those that came before us and shaped our lives to make us the people that we are today.

Table of Contents

Introduction

This is a compilation of individuals who lived in the Gaard of Skjerven, in the Municipality of Vik, in the County of Sogn og Fjordane, in the country of Norway from 1669 to 1922. I have placed each entry into one of four categories: Families, Individual Births/Baptisms, Individual Burials, and Individual Marriages. If the entry concerns an Individual who is female, then I have placed that person in the category of Individual Marriages. If the entry concerns an Individual who is male, then I have placed that person in the category of Individual Families. I have also decided to use the suffixes of –son, for male children, and –datter, for female children to make it easier for the reader to understand the relationship between child and parent. For example if a male child's name was Anders Larsson, the child would be Anders son of Lars, and if a female child's name was Britha Larsdatter, the child would be Britha daughter of Lars. Images of many of these listings are available at

http://digitalarkivet.uib.no/cgi-win/WebMeta.exe?slag=vismeny&fylkenr=14&knr=1417&aar=&dagens=&katnr=4

To help guide the reader of this work, the format of this book is as follows:

- **Main Family Entry (Husband and Wife) (Father and Mother)**

  - **Child of Main Family Entry, including Spouse(s) when available**

    - **Grandchild of Main Family Entry, including Spouse(s) when available**

      - **Great-Grandchild of Main Family Entry, including Spouse(s) when available**

(**Bolded Text**) following any entry includes any additional information such as Residence(s), Occupation(s), Signature(s), etc. when available.

Skjerven Gaard Vik Sogn og Fjordane Norway: 1669 to 1922

Some of the fonts used in this work symbolizes German Gothic writing, which was used in the church registers. The traditional letters, numbers, and punctuation marks and their German Gothic counterparts are as follows:

Traditional Letters (Uppercase & Lowercase)

A a B b C c D d E f G g H h I i J j K k L l M m

N n O o P p Q q R r S s T t U u V v W w X x Y y Z z

German Gothic Letters (Uppercase & Lowercase)

A a B b C c D d E e F f G g H h I i J j K k L l M m

N n O o P p Q q R r S s T t U u V v W w X x Y y Z z

Hurst

Traditional Numbers

1 2 3 4 5 6 7 8 9 10

German Gothic Numbers

1 2 3 4 5 6 7 8 9 10

Traditional Punctuation

. , : ' " & - ( )

German Gothic Punctuation

. , : ' " & - ( )

Families

- Aamund Olsson (1st Marriage) & Synneva Joendatter – 23 Jun 1743

  o Ingeborg Aamunddatter – b. 16 Sep 1744

Aamund Olsson (father):

Residence – Hatlestad, Leikanger – June 23, 1743

Synneva Joendatter (mother):

Residence – Skjerven, Vik – June 23, 1743

- Aamund Olsson (2nd Marriage) & Ragnhild Lassedatter (2nd Marriage) – 8 Dec 1775

Aamund Olson (husband):

Residence – Skjerven, Vik – December 8, 1775

Ragnhild Lassesdatter (wife):

Residence – Stedje, Vik – December 8, 1775

- Anders Endreson, b. 17 Jun 1767, d. 19 Jul 1857 & Britha Ellingdatter, b. 28 May 1775, d. 1 Jan 1847 – 7 Jun 1793
  - Endre Andersson – b. 12 May 1794, d. 18 Feb 1798
  - Elling Andersson – b. 25 Oct 1795, d. 18 May 1852 & Britha Olsdatter, b. 29 Jun 1806, d. 19 Oct 1889 – 15 Jun 1830
    - Britha Ellingdatter – b. 22 Nov 1832, chr. 25 Nov 1832, d. 6 Mar 1894

    ### Britha Ellingdatter (daughter):

    ### Christening – Hopperstad Parish

    - Ole Ellingson – b. 27 Jan 1837, chr. 29 Jan 1837 & Gjertrud Olsdatter, b. 26 Sep 1856, chr. 12 Oct 1856, d. 10 Feb 1898 – 15 May 1877
      - Elling Olsson – b. 25 May 1878, chr. 23 Jun 1878 & Synneva Olsdatter, b. 1878
        - Olav Ellingson – b. 23 Feb 1904, chr. 3 Apr 1904
        - Odvar Ellingson – b. 5 Jul 1905, chr. 3 Sep 1905
        - Elling Ellingson – b. 5 Apr 1907, chr. 26 May 1907
        - Anders Ellingson – b. 3 Dec 1908, chr. 28 Feb 1909
        - Sigmund Ellingson – b. 27 Jan 1910, chr. 24 Apr 1910

o Gjermund Ellingson – b. 29 May 1914, chr. 23 Aug 1914

Elling Olsson (son):

    Occupation – Farmer – April 3, 1904

        September 3, 1905

        May 26, 1907

        February 28, 1909

        April 24, 1910

        August 23, 1914

- Ole Olsson – b. 15 Feb 1880, chr. 14 Mar 1880

- John Olsson – b. 3 Jan 1883, chr. 21 Jan 1883

- Britha Olsdatter – b. 8 Mar 1886

Ole Ellingson (son):

    Residence – Skjerven, Vik – May 15, 1877

    Occupation – Bachelor – May 15, 1877

        Farmer – May 15 1877

        June 23, 1878

        March 14, 1880

        January 21, 1883

        March 8, 1886

Birth Place – Skjerven, Vik

Christening – Hopperstad Church

Gjertrud Olsdatter, daughter of Ole Olsson & Gjertrud Frikdatter from Hopperstad (daughter-in-law):

Residence – Vik – May 15, 1877

Birth Place – Hopperstad, Vik

Christening – Hopperstad Church

Also Known As – Gjertrud Olsdatter Hopperstad

▪ Synneva Ellingdatter – b. 12 Mar 1841, chr. 14 Mar 1841 & Ellend Johnson, b. 1828 – 1 May 1865

Synneva Ellingdatter (daughter):

Residence – Skjerven, Vik – May 1, 1865

Birth Place – Skjerven, Vik

Christening – Hopperstad Parish

Also Known As – Synneva Ellingdatter Skjerven

Ellend Johnson (husband):

    Residence – Holstad, Vik – May 1, 1865

    Occupation – Bachelor – May 1, 1865

    Birth Place – Holstad, Vik

    Also Known As – Ellend Johnson Holstad

▪ Elling Ellingson – b. 5 Mar 1846, chr. 8 Mar 1846

    Elling Ellingson (son):

    Christening – Hopperstad Church

Elling Andersson (son):

    Residence – Skjerven, Vik – June 15, 1830

    Occupation – Bachelor – June 15, 1830

        Renter – November 25, 1832

        Farmer – January 29, 1837

        March 14, 1841

        March 8, 1846

    Birth Place – Skjerven, Vik

Britha Olsdatter, daughter of Ole Siurson & Helga Olsdatter from Sæbø (daughter-in-law):

> **Birth Place** – Sæbø, Vik
>
> **Cause of Death** – pneumonia
>
> **Also Known As** – Britha Olsdatter Sæbø

o Ragnhild Andersdatter – b. 30 Oct 1798

o Endre Andersson – b. 12 Jun 1801, d. 21 Jun 1860 & Kari Pederdatter, b. 1790, d. 26 Oct 1854 – 13 Jun 1827

- Britha Endredatter – b. 10 Jun 1828, chr. 15 Jun 1828, d. 13 Sep 1898

  Britha Endredatter (daughter):

  > **Cause of Death** – gored to death by bull
  >
  > **Christening** – Hopperstad Parish

- Peder Endreson – b. 30 Nov 1830, chr. 5 Dec 1830

  Peder Endreson (son):

  > **Christening** – Hopperstad Parish

- Anders Endreson – b. 31 Dec 1833, chr. 1 Jan 1834, d. 18 Sep 1906

Anders Endreson (son):

Cause of Death – asthma

Christening – Hopperstad Parish

Endre Andersson (son):

Occupation – Bachelor & Farmer's son – June 13, 1827

Farmer – June 10, 1828

November 30, 1830

January 1, 1834

Birth Place – Skjerven, Vik

Kari Pederdatter (daughter-in-law):

Birth Place – Skjerven, Vik

o Anfind Andersson – b. 9 Jul 1804 & Anna Johannesdatter, b. 12

   May 1810 – 10 Jun 1831

   ▪ Anders Anfindson – b. 17 Nov 1835, chr. 29 Nov 1835

   ▪ Britha Anfinddatter – b. 7 May 1840, chr. 17 May 1840

   ▪ Elling Anfindson – 20 Apr 1847, chr. 30 Apr 1847

   Elling Andfindson (son):

   Remarks about Birth – **twin to Endre Anfindson**

   Christening – **Hopperstad Church**

   ▪ Endre Anfindson – 20 Apr 1847, chr. 30 Apr 1847

   Endre Andfindson (son):

   Remarks about Birth – **twin to Elling Andfindson**

   Christening – **Hopperstad Church**

Anfind Andersson (son):

   Residence – **Skjerven, Vik** – **June 10, 1831**

   Voll, Vik – **November 17, 1835**

   May 7, 1840

   April 20, 1847

Occupation – Bachelor – June 10, 1831

Soldier – June 10, 1831

Renter – November 17, 1835

Farmer – May 7, 1840

April 20, 1847

Birth Place – Skjerven, Vik

Anna Johannesdatter, daughter of Johannes Iverson & Britha Lassedatter of Stokkebø (daughter-in-law):

Birth Place – Voll, Vik

o Anna Andersdatter – 16 Aug 1807

o Johannes Andersson – b. 2 Mar 1810, d. 5 Feb 1812

o Johannes Andersson – b. 27 Feb 1813, d. 30 May 1855

o Britha Andersdatter, b. 12 Nov 1815 & Erik Johannesson, b. 30 Oct
  1810 – 6 May 1834

  ▪ Erik Erikson – b. 26 Aug 1832, chr. 2 Sep 1832

    Erik Erikson (son):

    Remarks about Birth – illegitimate

    Christening – Hopperstad Parish

  ▪ Johannes Erikson – b. 10 Sep 1834, chr. 21 Sep 1834

    Johannes Erikson (son):

    Christening – Hopperstad Parish

  ▪ Britha Erikdatter – b. 18 Mar 1837, chr. 24 Mar 1837

    Britha Erikdatter (daughter):

    Christening – Hopperstad Parish

  ▪ Britha Erikdatter – b. 2 Apr 1840, chr. 15 Apr 1840

    Britha Erikdatter (daughter):

    Christening – Hopperstad Parish

  ▪ Anders Erikson – b. 22 Sep 1844, chr. 6 Oct 1844

    Anders Erikson (son):

    Christening – Hopperstad Church

- Erik Erikson – b. 22 May 1847, chr. 30 May 1847

    ### Erik Erikson (son):

    #### Christening – Hove Church

- Anna Erikdatter – b. 13 Apr 1850, chr. 5 May 1850

    ### Anna Erikdatter (daughter):

    #### Christening – Hopperstad Church

- Eli Erikdatter – b. 7 Mar 1853, d. 26 Mar 1853

    ### Eli Erikdatter (daughter):

    #### Baptism – at home

- Elling Erikson – b. 1 Feb 1854, chr. 5 Mar 1854

    ### Elling Erikson (son):

    #### Christening – Hove Church

- Johannes Erikson – b. 25 Jan 1857, chr. 1 Mar 1857

    ### Johannes Erikson (son):

    #### Christening – Hopperstad Parish

Britha Andersdatter (daughter):

Residence – Vik – May 6, 1834

Birth Place – Skjerven, Vik

Hurst

Erik Johannesson, son of Johannes Hermundson & Britha Erikdatter of Hopperstad (son-in-law):

Residence – Hopperstad – May 6, 1834

September 21, 1834

March 24, 1837

April 15, 1840

May 30, 1847

May 5, 1850

March 26, 1853

March 5, 1854

Occupation – Bachelor – September 2, 1832

May 6, 1834

Soldier – May 6, 1834

Smallholder, Cottager – September 21, 1834

March 24, 1837

April 15, 1840

May 5, 1850

Farmer – May 30, 1847

March 26, 1853

March 5, 1854

Birth Place – Hopperstad, Vik

Also Known As – Erich Johannesson Hopperstad

o Gjertrud Andersdatter – b. 19 Jun 1818

Gjertrud Andersdatter (daughter):

Baptism – Vangsnes Church by Chaplain Mr. Ludvig Daae

Anders Endreson, son of Endre Unknown from Voll, Vik (father):

Residence – Skjerven, Vik – June 7, 1793

Britha Ellingdatter, daughter of Elling Olsson & Anna Anfinddatter from Bø (mother):

Residence – Bø, Vik – June 7, 1793

Remarks about Birth – born May 21st

• Anders Hermundson & Johanna Joendatter – 28 Dec 1744

Anders Hermundson (husband):

Residence – Skjerven, Vik – December 28, 1744

Johanna Joendatter (wife):

Residence – Sæbø, Vik – December 28, 1744

Remarks about Marriage – bride 'pregnant'

- Anders Olstad & Britha Ellingdatter
  - Ole Andersson – b. 7 Mar 1773 & Ingeborg Olsdatter, b. 5 Jul 1788 – 8 Jan 1815
    - Anders Olsson – b. 10 Dec 1815
    - Ragnhild Olsdatter – b. 13 Dec 1818

Ole Andersson (son):

Residence – Skjerven, Vik – January 8, 1815

Dahle – December 10, 1815

December 13, 1818

Occupation – Soldier – January 8, 1815

Smallholder, Cottager – December 13, 1818

Remarks about Birth – illegitimate born March 6th

Ingeborg Olsdatter, daughter of Ole Vilhelmson & Ragnhild Jakobdatter of Hellen (daughter-in-law):

Residence – Hellen, Vik – January 8, 1815

- Anders Unknown & Unknown

  o Martha Andersdatter – b. 15 Jul 1759

- Anders Unknown & Unknown

  o Kari Andersdatter – b. 1 October 1764

- Axel Olsson, b. 1872 & Martha Heljedatter, b. 23 Nov 1874, chr. 6 Dec 1874

  o Helje Axelson – b. 29 Jun 1898, chr. 31 Jul 1898, d. 21 May 1899

  Helje Axelson (son):

   Remarks about Birth – illegitimate

   Cause of Death – pneumonia

Axel Olsson (father):

 Occupation – Bachelor – July 31, 1898

   Farmer – July 31, 1898

 As Known As – Axel Olsson Ovrid

Martha Heljedatter, daughter of Helje Iverson, b. 7 Dec 1829, chr. 20 Dec 1829, d. 23 Sep 1890 & Anna Heljedatter, b. 24 Mar 1851, chr. 4 Apr 1851, married on 30 Jun 1874, from Skjerven (mother).

- Botholph Ingebrigtson & Gietlau Larsdatter – 20 May 1798

  o Anna Botholpdatter – b. 8 Feb 1799

    ## Anna Botholphdatter (daughter):

    ## Remarks about Birth – illegitimate

  o Elling Botholphson, b. 1 Jun 1802 & Mette Marie Lijedahl, b. 27 Jul 1808 – 8 Apr 1834

    - Johan Benjamin Ellingson – b. 1829, d. 17 Jul 1829

    - Katrine Dorthea Ellingdatter – b. 23 Aug 1832, chr. 7 Oct 1832

      ## Katrine Dorthea Ellingdatter (daughter):

      ## Remarks about Birth – illegitimate

    - Gietlau Ellingdatter – b. 14 Dec 1834, chr. 25 Dec 1834

      ## Gietlau Ellingdatter (daughter):

      ## Christening – Hopperstad Parish

    - Botholph Ellingson – b. 19 Jun 1837, chr. 24 Jun 1837

      ## Botholph Ellingson (son):

      ## Christening – Hopperstad Parish

- Johan Benjamin Ellingson – b. 10 Apr 1839, chr. 13 Apr 1839 & Briteva Nielsdatter, b. 26 Jan 1837, chr. 29 Jan 1837 – 2 May 1864

  - Elling Johanson – b. 4 Sep 1863, chr. 27 Sep 1863

    Elling Johanson (son):

    Remarks about Birth – illegitimate

    Also Known As – Elling Johanson Fjærestad

  - Gjertrud Johandatter – b. 1 Apr 1866, chr. 29 Apr 1866

  - Niels Johanson – b. 23 Apr 1868, chr. 31 May 1868

  - Mari Johandatter – b. 30 Sep 1869, chr. 24 Oct 1869

  - Gietlau Johandatter – b. 21 Oct 1871

    Gietlau Johandatter (daughter):

    Baptism – at home, dead

    Remarks about Birth – twin to Botholph Johanson

  - Botholph Johanson – b. 21 Oct 1871, chr. 2 Dec 1871

    Botholph Johanson (son):

    Remarks about Birth – twin to Gietlau Johandatter

  - Olina Johandatter – b. 15 Sep 1873, chr. 9 Nov 1873

- Britha Johandatter – b. 12 Oct 1875, chr. 23 Nov 1875

- Johan Johanson – b. 9 Jan 1878, chr. 10 Feb 1878

- Johanna Johandatter – b. 19 Mar 1880, chr. 2 May 1880

Johan Benjamin Ellingson (son):

Christening – Hopperstad Parish

Residence – Fjærestad, Vik – September 27, 1863

Skjerven, Vik – May 2, 1864

Hopperstad, Vik – April 29, 1866

May 31, 1868

October 24, 1869

December 2, 1871

November 9, 1873

November 23, 1875

February 10, 1878

May 2, 1880

Hagen – April 29, 1866

February 10, 1878

May 2, 1880

Occupation – Bachelor – September 27, 1863

May 2, 1864

Farmer – April 29, 1866

May 31, 1868

October 24, 1869

December 2, 1871

November 9, 1873

November 23, 1875

February 10, 1878

May 2, 1880

Birth Place – Skjerven, Vik

Also Known As – Johan Ellingson Skjerven

Briteva Nielsdatter, daughter of Niels Bendixson & Gjertrud Iverdatter of Fjærestad (daughter-in-law):

Christening – Hopperstad Parish

Residence – Fjærestad, Vik – May 2, 1864

Birth Place – Fjærestad, Vik

Also Known As – Briteva Nielsdatter Fjærestad

- Botolph Ellingson – b. 25 Mar 1842, d. 25 Jun 1842

- Botolph Ellingson – b. 7 May 1843, d. 26 May, 1843

- Gjertrud Ellingdatter – b. 6 Oct 1844, chr. 10 Oct 1844

  ### Gjertrud Ellingdatter (daughter):

  ### Christening – Hopperstad Parish

- Britha Ellingdatter – b. 4 Feb 1847, chr. 14 Feb 1847

  ### Britha Ellingdatter (daughter):

  ### Christening – Hopperstad Church

- Hermann Ellingson – b. 1 Feb 1851, Chr. 16 Feb 1851

  ### Hermann Ellingson (son):

  ### Christening – Hopperstad Church

Elling Botholphson (son):

Occupation – Bachelor – October 7, 1832

April 8, 1834

Renter – December 25, 1834

June 24, 1837

April 13, 1839

Farmer – March 25, 1842

May 7, 1843

February 14, 1847

Smallholder, Cottager – October 10, 1844

February 16, 1851

Birth Place – Skjerven, Vik

Mette Marie Lijedahl, daughter of Johan Benjamin Lijedahl & Gjertrud Hermunddatter (daughter-in-law):

Birth Place – Hopperstad, Vik

o Ole Botolphson, b. 8 Jan 1805 & Britha Jakobdatter, b. 5 Nov 1810 – 24 Jul 1836

▪ Gietlau Olsdatter – b. 23 Sep 1836, chr. 24 Sep 1836

Gietlau Olsdatter (daughter):

Christening – Hopperstad Parish

▪ Jakob Peder Olsson – b. 15 Dec 1838, chr. 26 Dec 1838

Jakob Peder Olsson (son):

Christening – Kvamsøy Parish

▪ Synneva Olsdatter – b. 9 Sep 1842

- Hansine Olsdatter – b. 22 May 1845, chr. 14 Jun 1845

Hansine Olsdatter (daughter):

Christening – Arnafjord Parish

- Hansine Olsdatter – b. 10 Apr 1847, chr. 2 May 1847

Hansine Olsdatter (daughter):

Christening – Kvamsøy Church

- Britha Olsdatter – b. 4 Jan 1849, chr. 28 Jan 1849

Britha Olsdatter (daughter):

Christening – Kvamsøy Church

Ole Botholphson (son):

Residence – Skjerven, Vik – July 24, 1836

Nesse – December 26, 1838

June 14, 1845

Indre Nesse – September 9, 1842

May 2, 1847

January 28, 1849

Occupation – Bachelor – July 24, 1836

Militia – July 24, 1836

Skjerven Gaard Vik Sogn og Fjordane Norway: 1669 to 1922

Renter – September 24, 1836

Smallholder, Cottager – December 26, 1838

September 9, 1842

January 28, 1849

Farmer – May 2, 1847

Birth Place – Skjerven, Vik

Britha Jakobdatter, daughter of Jakob Hansson & Synneva Johannesdatter from Vulf (daughter-in-law):

Residence – Vik – July 24, 1836

Birth Place – Vikøyri, Vik

o Britha Botolphdatter – b. 4 Mar 1807

o Britha Botolphdatter – b. 28 Jun 1812

Botholph Ingebrigtson (father):

Residence – Skjerven, Vik – May 20, 1798

Hatlekollen, Vik – February 8, 1799

Occupation – Soldier – May 20, 1798

Gietlau Larsdatter (mother):

Residence – Hatlekollen, Vik – May 20, 1798

- Botholph Ingebrigtson & Gietlau Larsdatter – 8 Sep 1804

  o Ingebrigt Botholphson, b. 23 Mar 1819 & Ragnhild Olsdatter, b. 1830 – 12 Nov 1862

    ▪ Gielau Ingbrigtdatter – b. 13 May 1862, chr. 25 May 1862

      ## Gietlau Ingebrigtdatter (daughter):

      ### Remarks about Birth – illegitimate

      ### Also Known As – Gietlau Ingebrigtdatter Lilleøren

    ▪ Elsa Ingebrigtdatter – b. 19 Aug 1866, chr. 16 Sep 1866

    ▪ Britha Ingebrigtdatter – b. 8 May 1870, chr. 26 Jun 1870

    ## Ingebright Botholphson (son):

    ### Residence – Lilleøren, Vik – May 25, 1862

    Skjerven, Vik – November 12, 1862

    Vikøyri, Vik – September 16, 1866

    Tryti, Vik – June 26, 1870

    ### Occupation – Bachelor – May 25, 1862

    November 12, 1862

    Smallholder, Cottager – September 16, 1866

    June 26, 1870

    Birth Place – Skjerven, Vik

    Also Known As – Ingebrigt Botholphson Skjerven

Ragnhild Olsdatter (daughter-in-law):

    Residence – Lilleøren, Vik – November 12, 1862

    Birth Place – Lilleøren, Vik

    Also Known As – Ragnhild Olsdatter Lilleøren

- Guthorm Botholphson – b. 21 Jan 1822, chr. 22 Jan 1822 d. 29 Oct 1889 & Britha Halvordatter, b. 6 Mar 1828, chr. 9 Mar 1828 – 30 Dec 1856

  - Britha Guthormdatter – b. 8 Mar 1857, chr. 20 Mar 1857

  Britha Guthormdatter (daughter):

      Christening – Hopperstad Church

  - Synneva Guthormdatter – b. 15 Mar 1863, chr. 29 Mar 1863

  - Botholph Guthormson – b. 22 Dec 1865, chr. 31 Dec 1865 & Britha Pederdatter, b. 1863 – 6 Jun 1889

Hurst

Botholph Guthormson (son of Guthorm Botholphson & Britha Halvordatter):

    Residence – Skjerven, Vik – June 6, 1889

    Occupation – Bachelor – June 6, 1889

        Renter – June 6, 1889

    Birth Place – Skjerven, Vik

Britha Pederdatter (daughter-in-law):

    Residence – Vik – June 6, 1889

    Birth Place – Tenold, Vik

Guthorm Botholphson (son):

    Residence – Skjerven, Vik – December 30, 1856

    Occupation – Bachelor – December 30, 1856

        Smallholder, Cottager – March 20, 1857

            March 29, 1863

            December 31, 1865

    Birth Place – Skjerven, Vik

    Cause of Death – pneumonia

Also Known As – Guthorm Botholphson Skjerven

Guthorm Botholphson Hopperstad

Britha Halvordatter, daughter of Halvor Halvorson & Britha Johndatter (daughter-in-law):

Residence – Hopperstad, Vik – December 30, 1856

Birth Place – Hopperstad, Vik

Christening – Hopperstad Parish

Also Known As – Britha Halvordatter Hopperstad

o Guthorm Botholphson (2nd Marriage) & Synneva Halvordatter (1st Marriage)

▪ Botholph Guthormson – b. 23 Jan 1849, chr. 18 Feb 1849, d. 20 May 1849

Botholph Guthormson (son):

Christening – Hopperstad Church

Remarks about Birth – illegitimate

Also Known As – Botholph Guthormson Skjerven

Guthorm Botholphson (son of Botholph Ingebrigtson & Gietlau Larsdatter):

Occupation – Bachelor – February 18, 1849

Botholph Ingebrigtson (father):

> **Residence** – Skjerven, Vik – September 8, 1804

> **Occupation** – Farmer – March 23, 1819

>> **January 22, 1822**

Gietlau Larsdatter (mother):

> **Residence** – Vigøren, Vik – September 8, 1804

- Ellend Unknown & Unknown

    o Unknown Ellendson – b. 11 Jul 1735

    o Britha Ellenddatter – b. Jul 1737

    o Joen Ellendson – b. 12 Apr 1742, d. 27 May 1742

    Joen Ellendson (son):

    > **Remarks about Death** – age 7 days

    o Synneva Ellenddatter – b. 3 Aug 1743, d. 7 Jul 1800

    o Britha Ellenddatter – b. 21 May 1747

    o Helga Ellenddater – b. 30 Nov 1749, d. 15 Apr 1809

- Elling Olsson & Ingeborg Olsdatter – 13 Jun 1776

  o Ole Ellingson – b. 13 Feb 1778

Elling Olsson (father):

Residence – Bø, Vik – June 13, 1776

Ingeborg Olsdatter (mother):

Residence – Skjerven, Vik – June 13, 1776

- Endre Andersson & Britha Johandatter – 8 Jun 1792

Endre Andersson (husband):

Residence – Skjerven, Vik – June 8, 1792

Britha Johandatter (wife):

Residence – Seim, Vik – June 8, 1792

- Erik Albrigtson & Botilla Siurdatter

  o Siur Erikson – b. 2 Feb 1789

  ### Siur Erikson (son):

  Remarks about Birth – illegitimate

Erik Albertson (father):

Remarks – "Erich Albertsen Skejerven of the young crew…"

- Erik Albrigtson & Britha Erikdatter – 18 Jun 1796

  o Albrigt Erikson, b. 15 Dec 1797 & Gjertrud Hermunddatter, b. 1796 – 28 Nov 1821

    ▪ Erik Albrigtson – b. 13 Aug 1822, chr. 14 Aug 1822, d. 29 Aug 1822

    ▪ Erik Albrigtson – b. 16 Dec 1823, chr. 21 Dec 1823 & Aase Olsdatter, b. 18 Sep 1814 – 3 Jun 1850

      • Johanna Erikdatter – b. 15 Jun 1848, chr. 4 Jul 1848

        Johanna Erikdatter (daughter):

        Christening – Hove Church

        Remarks about Birth – illegitimate

        Also Known As – Johanna Erikdatter Hopperstad

      • Ole Erikson – b. 18 Jan 1850, chr. 3 Feb 1850

        Ole Erichson (son):

        Remarks about Birth – illegitimate

      • Ole Erikson – b. 31 Jan 1851, chr. 16 Feb 1851

        Ole Erikson (son):

        Christening – Hopperstad Church

Erik Albrigtson (son):

Residence – Hopperstad, Vik – July 4, 1848

February 3, 1850

February 16, 1851

Skjerven, Vik – June 3, 1850

Occupation – Bachelor – July 4, 1848

February 3, 1850

June 3, 1850

Soldier – June 3, 1850

Renter – February 16, 1851

Birth Place – Skjerven, Vik

Also Known As – Erik Albrigtson Skjerven

Aase Olsdatter, daughter of Ole Joenson & Martha Fredrikdatter of Hopperstad (daughter-in-law):

Residence – Hopperstad, Vik – June 3, 1850

Birth Place – Hopperstad, Vik

Also Known As – Aase Olsdatter Hopperstad

- Hermund Albrigtson – b. 19 Dec 1825, chr. 25 Dec 1825

  ### Hermund Albrigtson (son):

  #### Christening – Hopperstad Parish

- Britha Albrigtdatter – b. 2 Dec 1829, chr. 25 Dec 1829

  ### Britha Albrigtdatter (daughter):

  #### Christening – Hopperstad Parish

- Ole Albrigtson – b. 8 Mar 1832, chr. 25 Mar 1832

  ### Ole Albrigtson (son):

  #### Christening – Hopperstad Parish

- Guthorm Albrigtson – b. 15 May 1835, chr. 17 May 1835

  ### Guthorm Albrigtson (son):

  #### Christening – Hopperstad Parish

- Martha Albrigtdatter – b. 23 Jun 1838, chr. 15 Jul 1838

  ### Martha Albrigtdatter (daughter):

  #### Christening – Hopperstad Parish

Albrigt Erikson (son):

Residence – Skjerven, Vik – November 28, 1821

Occupation – Bachelor – November 28, 1821

Farmer – August 13, 1822

December 2, 1829

March 25, 1832

Smallholder, Cottager – December 16, 1823

December 25, 1825

May 17, 1835

July 15, 1838

Birth Place – Skjerven, Vik

Social Status – Peasantry – November 28, 1821

Gjertrud Hermunddatter, (daughter-in-law):

Birth Place – Vikøren, Vik

Hurst

- Gjøri Erikdatter – b. 4 May 1803

- Niels Erikson, b. 16 Mar 1806 & Ingeborg Christendatter, b. 1809 – 24 Mar 1836

Niels Erikson (son):

    Residence – Skjerven, Vik – March 24, 1836

    Occupation – Bachelor – March 24, 1836

        Militia – March 24, 1836

    Birth Place – Skjerven, Vik

Ingeborg Christendatter (daughter-in-law):

    Residence – Vik – March 24, 1836

    Birth Place – Vangsnes, Vik

- Guthorm Erikson – b. 23 Feb 1809, d. 28 Nov 1832

Guthorm Erikson (son):

    Occupation – Bachelor – November 28, 1832

        Soldier – November 28, 1832

Skjerven Gaard Vik Sogn og Fjordane Norway: 1669 to 1922

Erik Albrigtson (father):

 Residence – Skjerven, Vik – June 18, 1796

 Occupation – Smallholder, Cottager – December 15, 1797

Britha Erikdatter (mother):

 Residence – Sæbø, Vik – June 18, 1796

- Erik Andersson & Britha Erikdatter
  - Synneva Erikdatter – b. 16 Sep 1795
- Erik Erikson, b. 14 Dec 1829, chr. 20 Dec 1829 & Martha Iverdatter, b. 8 Jul 1841, chr. 11 Jul 1841 – 12 Jun 1865
  - Ragnhild Erikdatter – b. 13 Jan 1865, chr. 15 Jan 1865, d. 30 Jan 1865

    Ragnhild Erikdatter (daughter):

     Remarks about Birth – illegitimate

     Remarks about Death – illegitimate child

     Also Known As – Ragnhild Erikdatter Skjerven
  - Anna Erikdatter – b. 15 Mar 1866, chr. 1 Apr 1866
  - Ragnhild Erikdatter – b. 12 Jul 1868, chr. 19 Jul 1868
  - Iver Erikson – b. 14 Mar 1871, chr. 9 Apr 1871

o Erik Erikson – b. 2 Jul 1873, chr. 2 Jul 1873

o Anna Erikdatter – b. 26 Oct 1883, chr. 25 Nov 1883

o Ole Erikson – b. 24 Oct 1887, chr. 11 Dec 1887

Erik Erikson, son of Erik Iverson & Ragnhild Andersdatter (father):

Residence – Tryti, Vik – June 12, 1865

April 1, 1866

Tistel, Vik – July 19, 1868

April 9, 1871

July 2, 1873

November 25, 1883

December 11, 1887

Occupation – Bachelor – January 15, 1865

June 12, 1865

Farmer – April 1, 1866

July 19, 1868

April 9, 1871

July 2, 1873

November 25, 1883

December 11, 1887

Skjerven Gaard Vik Sogn og Fjordane Norway: 1669 to 1922

Birth Place – Tryti, Vik

Christening – Hopperstad Parish

Also Known As – Erik Erikson Tryti

Martha Iverdatter, daughter of Iver Heljeson & Anna Olsdatter of Bø (mother):

Residence – Skjerven, Vik – June 12, 1865

Birth Place – Skjerven, Vik

Also Known As – Martha Iverdatter Skjerven

- Gabriel Larsson, b. 14 Sep 1870 & Kari Larsdatter, b. 9 Mar 1874 – 1 May 1900

  o Marie Gabrieldatter – b. 26 Dec 1900, chr. 3 Feb 1901

    Marie Gabrieldatter (daughter):

      Also Known As – Marie Gabrieldatter Mundal

  o Lars Gabrielson – b. 8 Sep 1903, chr. 25 Oct 1903

  o Siur Gabrielson – b. 26 Apr 1909, chr. 16 Jun 1909

    Siur Gabrielson (son):

      Baptism – at home

  o Lovisa Gabrieldatter – b. 6 Jul 1912, chr. 13 Oct 1912

Gabriel Larsson, son of Lars Otheson & Johanna Gjertdatter of Løfall, Gaular (father):

Residence – **Løfald, Sunnfjord – May 1, 1900**

Skjerven, Vik – February 3, 1901

Bø, Vik – February 3, 1901

Brudevoll, Vik – October 25, 1903

Vikøren, Vik – June 16, 1909

Sæbø, Vik – October 13, 1912

Occupation – **Servant – February 3, 1901**

Smallholder, Cottager – October 25, 1903

Worker – June 16, 1909

October 13, 1912

Birth Place – **Løfald, Sunnfjord**

As Known As – **Gabriel Larsson Bø**

Kari Larsdatter, daughter of Lars Larsson & Malena Siurdatter of Mundal, Balestrand (mother):

Residence – Mundal, Balestrand – May 1, 1900

Birth Place – Mundal Balestrand

- Guthorm Ellingson & Anna Pederdatter – 17 Jun 1775

Guthorm Ellingson (husband):

Residence – Skjerven, Vik – June 17, 1775

Anna Pederdatter (wife):

Residence – Tryti, Vik – June 17, 1775

- Guthorm Ingebrigtson & Gietlau Larsdatter

   o   Britha Guthormdatter – b. 6 Jan 1816

- Hans Hansson & Anna Botholphdatter – 18 May 1820

  o Lars Hansson – b. 23 Jan 1820

    ## Lars Hansson (son):

      ### Remarks about Birth – illegitimate

  o Siur Hansson – b. 11 Dec 1821, chr. 16 Dec 1821

  o Siur Hansson – b. 10 Oct 1825, chr. 16 Oct 1825

    ## Siur Hansson (son):

      ### Christening – Hopperstad Parish

Hans Hansson (father):

Residence – Gilderhuus – May 18, 1820

January 23, 1820

December 16, 1821

October 16, 1825

Grov – October 16, 1825

Occupation – Smallholder, Cottager – October 16, 1825

Anna Botholphdatter (mother):

Residence – Skjerven, Vik – May 18, 1820

- Hans Johannesson & Martha Olsdatter – 26 Apr 1783

Hans Johannesson (husband):

Residence – Skjerven, Vik – April 26, 1783

Occupation – Soldier – April 26, 1783

Martha Olsdatter (wife):

Residence – Føli, Vik – April 26, 1783

Remarks at Marriage – bride from Vikøyri

- Helje Iverson, b. 7 Dec 1829, chr, 20 Dec 1829, d. 23 Sep 1890 & Anna Heljedatter, b. 24 Mar 1851, chr. 4 Apr 1851 – 30 Jun 1874

  o Iver Heljeson – b. 24 Nov 1874, d. 29 Nov 1874

  ### Iver Heljeson (son):

  ### Christening – the home, dead

  o Martha Heljedatter – b. 23 Nov 1874, chr. 6 Dec 1874

  o Iver Heljeson – b. 15 Jan 1877, chr. 4 Feb 1877

  o Britha Heljedatter – b. 29 Jul 1879, chr. 24 Aug 1879

  o Helje Heljeson – b. 18 Feb 1881, chr. 20 Mar 1881

  o Ole Heljeson – b. 5 May 1884, chr. 15 Jun 1884

o Sigtona Heljedatter – b. 11 Jun 1886, chr. 17 Jun 1886, d. 17 Jun 1886

Sigtona Heljedatter (daughter):

Christening – at home, dead

o Peder Heljeson – b. 6 Nov 1887, chr. 11 Dec 1887

Helje Iverson, son of Iver Heljeson Ovrid & Martha Olsdatter from Bø (father):

Residence – Skjerven, Vik – June 30, 1874

Occupation – Bachelor – June 30, 1874

Farmer – June 30, 1874

December 6, 1874

February 4, 1877

August 24, 1879

March 20, 1881

June 15, 1884

June 17, 1886

December 11, 1887

Birth Place – Skjerven, Vik

Christening – Hove Parish

Remarks about Birth – illegitimate

Also Known As – Helje Iverson Bø

Anne Heljedatter, daughter of Helje Anderson & Martha Arnedatter from Ovrid (mother):

Residence – Vik – June 30, 1874

Birth Place – Ovrid, Vik

Christening – Hopperstad Church

- Henrik Lasseson & Britha Lassedatter

  o Botholph Henrikson – b. 26 Sep 1857, chr. 4 Oct 1857

  Botholph Henrikson (son):

  Remarks about Birth – illegitimate

  Also Known As – Botholph Henrikson Skjerven

Henrik Lasseson (father):

Occupation – Bachelor – October 4, 1857

Also Known As – Henrik Lasseson Sæbø

- Hermund Ingebrigtson & Alis Hermunddatter – 8 Jun 1800

  o Britha Hermunddatter – b. 21 Jan 1802

  o Ole Hermundson – b. 11 Jun 1805

  o Thuri Hermunddatter – b. 17 Jan 1809

  o Ingebrigt Hermundson – b. 22 Apr 1811

  o Ole Hermundson – b. 5 Jan 1815

  o Inger Hermunddatter – b. 23 Jun 1824, chr. 30 Jun 1824

Hermund Ingebrigtson (father):

Residence – Skjerven, Vik – June 8, 1800

January 21, 1802

Fjærestad, Vik – June 11, 1805

April 22, 1811

January 5, 1815

June 30, 1824

Haalane, Vik – January 17, 1809

Occupation – Soldier – June 8, 1800

Smallholder, Cottager – June 30, 1824

Alis Hermunddatter (mother):

Residence – Steje, Vik – June 8, 1800

- Hermund Ingebrigtson & Britha Jensdatter

  o Jens Hermundson – b. 4 Oct 1797

    Jens Hermundson (son):

      Remarks about Birth – illegitimate

Hermund Ingebrigtson (father):

  Residence – Skjerven – October 4, 1797

- Hermund Johannesson, b. 21 Feb 1818 & Anna Endredatter, b. 1822, d. 4 Apr 1890 – 12 Jan 1848

  o Johannes Hermundson – b. 18 Jun 1846, chr. 21 Jun 1846, d. 21 Apr 1888 & Sigrid Hermunddatter, b. 9 Oct 1850, chr. 3 Nov 1850 – 17 Jun 1884

    ▪ Hermund Johannesson – b. 8 Feb 1885, chr. 1 Mar 1885

    ▪ Anna Johannesdatter – b. 4 Mar 1887, chr. 3 Apr 1887, d. 23 Jan 1889

      Anna Johannesdatter (daughter):

        Cause of Death – blood poisoning

Johannes Hermundson (son):

Residence – Skjerven, Vik – June 17, 1884

Occupation – Bachelor – June 17, 1884

Farmer – June 17, 1884

March 1, 1885

April 3, 1887

Christening – Hopperstad Church

Remarks about Birth – illegitimate

Birth Place – Skjerven, Vik

Cause of Death – encephalitis

Sigrid Hermunddatter, daughter of Hermund Siurson & Ingeborg Johndatter from Risløv (daughter-in-law):

Residence – Vik – June 17, 1884

Christening – Hove Church

Birth Place – Risløv, Vik

o Endre Hermundson – b. 17 Feb 1848, chr. 5 Mar 1848, d. 20 Apr 1848

Endre Hermundson (son):

Christening – Hove Church

o Kari Hermunddatter – b. 3 Oct 1849, chr. 21 Oct 1849

Kari Hermunddatter (daughter):

Christening – Hopperstad Church

o Endre Hermundson – b. 5 Nov 1853, chr. 13 Nov 1853

Endre Hermundson (son):

Christening – Hopperstad Church

o Peder Hermudson – b. 19 Jul 1856, d. 31 Jul 1856

Peder Hermundson (son):

Christening – at home

o Britha Hermunddatter – b. 15 Feb 1858, chr. 21 Feb 1858

o Synneva Hermunddatter – 16 Jul 1860, chr. 22 Jul 1860

o Peder Hermundson – b. 26 Mar 1863, chr. 5 Apr 1863 & Johanna Anfinddatter, b. 20 Feb 1865, chr. 12 Mar 1865 – 29 Jun 1892

  ▪ Hermund Pederson – b. 3 Dec 1892, chr. 15 Jan 1893

Peder Hermundson (son):

Residence – Skjervan, Vik – June 29, 1892

Occupation – Bachelor – June 29, 1892

Farmer – June 29, 1892

January 15, 1893

Birth Place – Skjerven, Vik

Also Known As – Peder Hermundson Skjerven

Johanna Anfinddatter, daughter of Anfind Johannesson & Martha Guthormdatter from Brekke (daughter-in-law):

Birth Place – Brekke, Vik

Also Known As – Johanna Anfinddatter Brekke

Hermund Johannesson, son of Johannes Hermundson & Britha Erikdatter of Hopperstad (father):

Residence – Hopperstad, Vik – January 12, 1848

October 21, 1849

Occupation – Bachelor – January 12, 1848

Renter – March 5, 1848

October 21, 1849

Farmer – November 15, 1853

July 31, 1856

February 21, 1858

July 22, 1860

April 5, 1863

Birth Place – Hopperstad, Vik

Anna Endredatter (mother):

Residence – Skjerven, Vik – January 12, 1848

Birth Place – Skjerven, Vik

- Ingebrigt Ingebrigtson & Martha Larsdatter – 31 May 1812

  o Britha Ingebrigtdatter – b. 20 Jun 1812

  o Lars Ingebrigtson – b. 19 Mar 1815

  o Britha Ingebrigtdatter – b. 16 Dec 1821, chr. 22 Dec 1821

Ingebrigt Ingebrigtson (father):

Residence – Skjerven, Vik – May 31, 1812

Sæbø, Vik – March 19, 1815

Vigøren, Vik – December 22, 1821

Occupation – Smallholder, Cottager – December 22, 1821

Martha Larsdatter (mother):

Residence – Vigøren, Vik – May 31, 1812

- Ingebrigt Olsson & Britha Hermunddatter – 22 Jun 1765
  - Ole Ingebrigtson – b. 11 Sep 1766, d. 12 Jun 1804
  - Hermund Ingebrigtson – b. 17 Nov 1769
  - Botholph Ingebrigtson – b. 12 Apr 1772

    #### Botholph Ingebrigtson (son):

    ##### Remarks – born April 6th

  - Ingebrigt Ingebrigtson – b. 16 Apr 1775

    #### Ingebrigt Ingebrigtson (son):

    ##### Remarks – born April 9th

Ingebrigt Olsson (father):

Residence – Skjerven, Vik – June 22, 1765

Birth Place – Vik

Britha Hermunddatter (mother):

Residence – Midlang, Vik – June 22, 1765

Birth Place – Vik

- Iver Johnson, b. 22 Mar 1814 & Synneva Rolanddatter, b. 1818 – 1 May 1843

  o Britha Iverdatter – b. 14 Sep 1842

  ### Britha Iverdatter (daughter):

  #### Remarks about Birth – illegitimate

  o John Iverson – b. 29 Mar 1844, chr. 7 Apr 1844

  ### John Iverson (son):

  #### Christening – Hove Parish

  o Ragnhild Iverdatter – b. 24 Dec 1846, chr. 28 Dec 1846

  ### Ragnhild Iverdatter (daughter):

  #### Christening – Hopperstad Church

Iver Johnson, son of John Lasseson & Britha Iverdatter from Orvdal (father):

Residence – Skjerven, Vik – September 14, 1842

Orvedal, Vik – May 1, 1843

April 7, 1844

December 28, 1846

Occupation – Bachelor – September 14, 1842

May 1, 1843

Militia – May 1, 1843

Smallholder, Cottager – April 7, 1844

December 28, 1846

Remarks – From Orvedal

Synneva Rolanddatter (mother):

Residence – Vik – May 1, 1843

Birth Place – Skjerven, Vik

- Joen Andersson & Anna Johannesdatter – 3 Jul 1780
  - Johannes Joenson – b. 13 Jan 1781

Joen Andersson (father):

Residence – Skjerven, Vik – July 3, 1780

Vange, Vik – January 13, 1781

Occupation – Soldier – July 3, 1780

Anna Johannesdatter (wife):

Residence – Hopperstad, Vik – July 3, 1780

- Joen Arneson & Ragnhild Olsdatter

  o Unknown Joendatter – b. 2 Jul 1732

    Unknown Joendatter (daughter):

      Remarks about Birth – illegitimate

Joen Arneson (father):

Remarks – From Seimsøyri

- Joen Pederson & Britha Ellingdatter – 27 Dec 1814

  o Kari Joendatter – b. 19 Feb 1815

  o Peder Joenson – b. 21 Feb 1818

Joen Pederson (father):

Residence – Skjerven, Vik – December 27, 1814

Tryti, Vik – February 19, 1815

February 21, 1818

Occupation – Militia – December 27, 1814

Britha Ellingdatter (mother):

Residence – Tryti, Vik – December 27, 1814

- Johannes Unknown & Unknown

  o Anna Johannesdatter – b. 22 Nov 1742, d. 2 Feb 1743

  ### Anna Johannesdatter (daughter):

  #### Remarks about Death – age 6 days

  o Lasse Johannesson – b. 24 Jun 1744

  o Anna Johannesdatter – b. 24 Apr 1747

  o Hans Johannesson – b. 1 Aug 1751

- John Johannesson, b. 12 Jan 1824, chr. 13 Jan 1824 & Kari Endredatter, b. 13 Jun 1824, chr. 15 Jun 1824 – 28 Dec 1846

  o Endre Johnson – b. 13 Jan 1850, chr. 3 Feb 1850

  ### Endre Johnson (son):

  #### Christening – Hopperstad Church

John Johannesson, son of Johannes Hermundson & Britha Erikdatter from Hopperstad (father):

Residence – Hopperstad, Vik – December 28, 1846

Occupation – Bachelor – December 28, 184

Farmer – December 28, 1846

Renter – February 3, 1850

Birth Place – Hopperstad, Vik

Remarks about Birth – twin

Also Known As – John Johannesson Hopperstad

Kari Endredatter, daughter of Endre Olsson & Luci Thordatter from Holstad (daughter-in-law):

Residence – Holstad, Vik – December 28, 1846

Birth Place – Holstad, Vik

Remarks about Birth – illegitimate

Also Known As – Kari Endredatter Hagen

- Lars Andersson & Britha Ellingdatter – 28 Dec 1778

  o Gietlau Larsdatter – b. 1 Feb 1778

  Gietlau Larsdatter (daughter):

  Remarks about Birth – illegitimate

  o Britha Larsdatter – b. 1 Nov 1782

  o Martha Larsdatter – b. 5 Feb 1787

Hurst

Lars Andersson (father):

Residence – Seim, Vik – December 28, 1778

Occupation – Soldier – February 1, 1778

December 28, 1778

Remarks – From Seimsøyri, Vetløyri

Britha Ellingdatter (mother):

Residence – Skjerven, Vik – December 28, 1778

• Lars Larsson & Kari Rolanddatter – 22 Jul 1810

  o Ole Larsson – b. 24 Jan 1810

Ole Larsson (son):

Remarks about Birth – illegitimate

Lars Larsson (father):

Residence – Qvame, Vik – July 22, 1810

Skidtvigen – January 24, 1810

Remarks – "Father Lars Larsen Skidtvigen servant of Elling Qvame"

Kari Rolanddatter (mother):

Residence – Qvame, Vik – July 22, 1810

- Ludvig Jørgen Johan Larsson, b. 1815 & Florentine Caroline Larsdatter, b. 1815 – 24 Jan 1841

  o Anna Mari Ludvigdatter – b. 11 May 1841, chr. 14 Oct 1841

  ### Anna Mari Ludvigdatter (daughter):

  #### Christening – Hopperstad Parish

  o Lars Ludvigson – b. 6 Oct 1842

Ludvig Jørgen Johan Larsson, son of Lars Skage (father):

Residence – Kvamsøy, Balestrand – January 24, 1841

Occupation – Rural Store Owner – January 24, 1841

Birth Place – Bergen, Bergen

Remarks about Marriage – married in Leikanger Parish

Also Known As – Ludvig Jørgen Johan Larsson Skage

Florentine Caroline Larsdatter, daughter of Lars Holter (mother):

Residence – Skau, Leikanger – January 24, 1841

Birth Place – Drammen, Drammen

Also Known As – Florentine Caroline Larsdatter Holter

- Niels Monsson & Anna Siurdatter

  o Ingebor Nielsdatter – b. 11 Oct 1807, d. 14 Oct 1828

  o Kristi Nielsdatter – b. 23 Jan 1811, d. 7 May 1811

  ### Kristi Nielsdatter (daughter):

  ### Age at Death – 3 months, 3 weeks

  o Kristi Nielsdatter – b. 20 Feb 1813

  o Ole Nielsson – b. 12 Apr 1817 & Gjertrud Olsdatter, b. 18 Oct 1817

  – 5 Jun 1848

  - Anna Olsdatter – b. 12 Aug 1847, chr. 22 Aug 1847

  ### Anna Olsdatter (daughter):

  ### Christening – Hove Church

  ### Remarks about Birth – illegitimate

  ### Also Known As – Anna Olsdatter Bø

- Ole Olsson – b. 22 Dec 1849, chr. 6 Jan 1850

Ole Olsson (son):

Christening – Hove Church

- Elling Olsson – b. 15 Jan 1852, chr. 8 Feb 1852

Elling Olsson (son):

Christening – Hove Church

- Niels Olsson – b. 17 Oct 1854, chr. 22 Oct 1854

Niels Olsson (son):

Christening – Hopperstad Church

- Iver Olsson – b. 13 Nov 1857, chr. 15 Nov 1857

Ole Nielsson (son):

Residence – Bø, Vik – August 22, 1847

Skjerven, Vik – June 5, 1848

Stadheim, Vik – January 6, 1850

Fjærestad, Vik – February 8, 1852

October 22, 1854

November 15, 1857

Hurst

Occupation – Bachelor – August 22, 1847

June 5, 1848

Farmer – August 22, 1847

Renter – January 6, 1850

Smallholder, Cottager – February 8, 1852

October 22, 1854

November 15, 1857

Birth Place – Skjerven, Vik

Also Known As – Ole Nielsson Skjerven

Gjertrud Olsdatter, daughter of Ole Guthormson & Martha Olsdatter from Bø (daughter-in-law):

Residence – Bø, Vik – June 5, 1848

Birth Place – Bø, Vik

- Ole Ingebrigtson & Anna Siurdatter – 12 Feb 1791

    o Ingebrigt Olsson – b. 5 Jan 1792

    o Britha Olsdatter – b. 22 Feb 1796

    o Gjertrud Olsdatter (2nd Marriage), b. 20 Feb 1799 & Hermund Siurson (2nd Marriage), b. Apr 1790 – 7 Nov 1848

Gjertrud Olsdatter (daughter):

Residence – Skjerven, Vik – November 7, 1848

Birth Place – Skjerven, Vik

Also Known As – Gjertrud Olsdatter Skjerven

Hermund Siurson, son of Siur Hermundson & Martha Arnedatter from Hopperstad (son-in-law):

Residence – Vikøren, Vik – November 7, 1848

Relationship Status at Marriage – widow

Birth Place – Hopperstad, Vik

Also Known As – Hermund Siurson Hopperstad

○ Bohilda Olsdatter – b. 13 Nov 1801, d. 31 Mar 1844

○ Britha Olsdatter – b. 1 Dec 1804

Ole Ingebrigtson (father):

Residence – Skjerven, Vik – February 12, 1791

Anna Siurdatter (mother):

Residence – Fjærestad, Vik – February 12, 1791

- Ole Iverson, b. 1846 & Dordei Olsdatter, b. 1846 – 30 Jun 1886

  o Ole Olsson – b. 5 Nov 1884, chr. 14 Nov 1884

  Ole Olsson (son):

  Christening – the home

  Remarks about Birth – illegitimate

  o Iver Olsson – b. 8 Feb 1887, chr. 14 Feb 1887, d. 15 Feb 1887

  Iver Olsson (son):

  Christening – the home, dead

  Remarks about Death – blow up

  o Iver Olsson – b. 20 Sep 1888, chr. 4 Nov 1888, d. 21 May 1892

Ole Iverson (father):

Residence – Skjerven, Vik – June 30, 1886

Occupation – Bachelor – November 14, 1884

Renter – November 14, 1884

February 14, 1887

November 4, 1888

Blacksmith – November 14, 1884

June 30, 1886

February 14, 1887

November 4, 1888

Birth Place – Skjerven, Vik

Dordei Olsdatter (mother):

Residence – Vik – June 30, 1886

Birth Place – Brekke, Balestrand

- Ole Nielsson, b. 1809 & Inger Olsdatter, b. 24 Aug 1811 – 31 Jan 1837

  o Niels Olsson – b. 4 Dec 1834, chr. 10 Dec 1834

  Niels Olsson (son):

  Christening – Hopperstad Parish

  Remarks about Birth – illegitimate

  o Martha Olsdatter – b. 25 Dec 1838, chr. 1 Jan 1839

  Martha Olsdatter (daughter):

  Christening – Hopperstad Parish

Ole Nielsson (father):

    Residence – Skjerven, Vik – January 31, 1837

        Tryti, Vik – January 1, 1839

    Occupation – Bachelor – December 10, 1834

        January 31, 1837

        Militia – January 31, 1837

        Smallholder, Cottager – January 1, 1839

    Birth Place – Skjerven, Vik

Inger Olsdatter, daughter of Ole Johannesson & Kari Johannesdatter from Hagen (mother):

    Residence – Vik – January 31, 1837

    Birth Place – Hagen, Vik

- Ole Pederson, b. 29 Jun 1828 & Martha Ingebrigtdatter (2nd Marriage), b. 1828, d. 1 Jan 1901 – 2 Jan 1862
  - Alice Olsdatter – b. 27 Mar 1858, chr. 4 Apr 1858

    Alice Olsdatter (daughter):

        Remarks About Birth – illegitimate

        Also Known As – Alice Olsdatter Vikøren

o   Gjertrud Olsdatter – b. 13 Sep 1860, chr. 7 Oct 1860

Gjertrud Olsdatter (daughter):

Remarks about Birth – illegitimate

Also Known As – Gjertrud Olsdatter Vikøren

o   Peder Olsson – b. 23 Dec 1863, chr. 17 Jan 1864

o   Ingebrigt Olsson – b. 30 Oct 1866, chr. 25 Dec 1866

Ole Pederson, son of Peder Johnson & Ragnhild Pederdatter from Hove (father):

Residence – Vikøyri, Vik – October 7, 1860

January 17, 1864

December 25, 1866

Skjerven, Vik – January 2, 1862

Occupation – Bachelor – April 4, 1858

October 7, 1860

January 2, 1862

Smallholder, Cottager – January 17, 1864

December 25, 1866

Birth Place – Skjerven, Vik

Also Known As – Ole Pederson Skjerven

Ole Pederson Grov

Martha Ingebrigtdatter (mother):

Residence – Vigøren, Vik – January 2, 1862

Birth Place – Vigøren, Vik

Cause of Death – stomach inflammation

Also Known As – Martha Ingebrigtdatter Vigøren

- Ole Siurson & Anna Johannesdatter
  - Johannes Olsson – b. 9 Mar 1802

    ### Johannes Olsson (son):

    Remarks about Birth – illegitimate

Ole Siurson (father):

Residence – Breyen – March 9, 1802

Anna Johannesdatter (mother):

Birth Place – Luster

- Ole Siurson & Synneva Larsdatter – 20 Jun 1799

  o Malena Olsdatter – b. 3 Oct 1803

  o Siur Olsson – b. 7 Sep 1806

  o Kari Olsdatter – b. 2 Oct 1809

  o Mikkel Olsson – b. 15 Nov 1812

  o Lars Olsson – b. 12 Feb 1816

  o Britha Olsdatter – b. 23 Oct 1819

    Britha Olsdatter (daughter):

      Christening – Hove Church

  o Britha Olsdatter – b. 7 Jan 1823, chr. 12 Jan 1823

Ole Siurson (father):

Residence – Skjerven, Vik – June 20, 1799

Vigøren, Vik – October 3, 1803

September 7, 1806

October 2, 1809

February 12, 1816

October 23, 1819

January 7, 1823

Brejen, Vik – November 15, 1812

Occupation – Smallholder, Cottager – October 23, 1819

January 7, 1823

Synneva Larsdatter (mother):

Residence – Vigøren, Vik – June 20, 1799

- Ole Vaasson & Unknown

  o Kari Olsdatter – b. 14 Dec 1757, d. 24 Dec 1758

  Kari Olsdatter (daughter):

  Age at Death – 1 year, 5 weeks, and 3 days

  o Unknown Olsdatter – b. Jul 1758

- Peder Andersson, b. 1747, d. 2 Mar 1826 & Synneva Joendatter – 15 Jun 1775

  o Roland Pederson – b. 2 Feb 1775, d. 28 Nov 1854 & Ragnhild Guthormdatter, b. 1786, d. 27 Jun 1862 – 13 Feb 1808

    ▪ Endre Rolandson – b. 16 Dec 1807 & Britha Botholphdatter, b. 28 Jun 1812 – 20 Feb 1845

      • Peder Endreson – b. 9 Mar 1843 & Ingerid Olsdatter, b. 28 Sep 1843 – 1 Nov 1867

        o Endre Pederson – b. 7 Mar 1867, chr. 31 Mar 1867

Endre Pederson (son):

Remarks about Birth – illegitimate

Also Known As – Endre Pederson Midlang

o Britha Pederdatter – b. 21 Jul 1868, chr. 16 Aug 1868, d. 22 Jul 1903

Britha Pederdatter (daughter):

Cause of Death – encephalitis

Also Known As – Britha Pederdatter Midlang

o Britha Pederdatter – b. 24 Nov 1869, chr. 9 Jan 1870

o Ole Pederson – b. 2 Sep 1871, chr. 8 Oct 1871

o Peder Pederson – b. 18 May 1873, chr. 1 Jun 1873

o Anna Pederdatter – b. 12 Feb 1875, chr. 28 Mar 1875

o Inger Pederdatter – b. 7 Mar 1877, chr. 1 Apr 1877

o Johanna Pederdatter – b. 16 Feb 1879, chr. 13 Apr 1879

o Iver Pederson – b. 5 Dec 1880, chr. 9 Dec 1880

o Synneva Pederdatter – b. 25 Nov 1881, chr. 25 Dec 1881

o Iver Pederson – b. 7 May 1884, chr. 1 Jun 1884

o Guthorm Pederson – b. 5 Aug 1886, chr. 12 Sep 1886

Hurst

Peder Endreson (son):

Residence – Midlang – March 31, 1867

March 28, 1875

April 7, 1877

April 13, 1879

December 9, 1880

December 25, 1881

June 1, 1884

September 12, 1886

Skjerven, Vik – November 1, 1867

Occupation – Bachelor – March 31, 1867

November 1, 1867

Farmer – August 16, 1868

January 9, 1870

October 8, 1871

June 1, 1873

March 28, 1875

April 1, 1877

April 13, 1879

70

December 9, 1880

December 25, 1881

June 1, 1884

September 12, 1886

Birth Place – Skjerven, Vik

Remarks about Birth – illegitimate

Also Known As – Peder Endreson Skjerven

Ingerid Olsdatter, daughter of Ole Hermundson & Aase Olsdatter from Midlang (daughter-in-law):

Birth Place – Midlang, Vik

- Ragnhild Endredatter – b. 10 Jan 1846, chr. 12 Jan 1846

Ragnhild Endredatter (daughter):

Christening – Hove Church

- Botholph Endreson – b. 12 May 1848, chr. 19 May 1848, d. 16 Nov 1848

Botholph Endreson (son):

Christening – Hove Church

Hurst

- Ragnhild Endredatter, b. 24 May 1851, chr. 8 Jun 1851 &

  Guthorm Johnson, b. 1 Dec 1850 – 9 Jun 1875

  o John Guthormson – b. 21 Dec 1873, chr. 1 Jan 1874

    John Guthormson (son):

      Remarks about Birth – illegitimate

    Ragnhild Endredatter (daughter):

      Residence – Vik – June 9, 1875

      Christening – Hopperstad Church

      Birth Place – Skjerven, Vik

    Guthorm Johnson, son of John Guthormson & Ingeborg Johndatter

    of Fosse, Vik (son-in-law):

      Residence – Fjærestad, Vik – June 9, 1875

      Occupation – Bachelor – January 1, 1874

                        June 9, 1875

                Joiner – January 1, 1874

      Christening – Hopperstad Church

      Birth Place – Fosse, Vik

      Also Known As – Guthorm Johnson Fjærestad

- Botolph Endreson – b. 25 Jan 1855, chr. 28 Jan 1855, d. 5

  Jul 1862

  Botolph Endreson (son):

  Christening – Hopperstad Church

Endre Rolandson (son):

  Residence – Skjerven, Vik – February 20, 1845

  Occupation – Bachelor – March 9, 1843

  February 20, 1845

  Farmer – January 12, 1846

  Renter – May 19, 1848

  Smallholder, Cottager – June 8, 1851

  January 28, 1855

  Birth Place – Skjerven, Vik

Britha Botolphdatter, daughter of Botolph Ingebrigtson & Gietlau Larsdatter (daughter-in-law):

  Residence – Vik – February 20, 1845

  Birth Place – Skjerven, Vik

■ Peder Rolandson – b. 11 Sep 1825, chr. 18 Sep 1825

Peder Rolandson (son):

Christening – Hopperstad Parish

Roland Pederson (father):

Residence – Skjerven, Vik – February 13, 1808

Occupation – Soldier – February 13, 1808

Militia – February 13, 1808

Smallholder, Cottager – September 18, 1825

Remarks – born January 27th

Remarks about Birth – illegitimate

Ragnhild Guthormdatter (mother):

Residence – Hønsi, Vik – February 13, 1808

○ Anders Pederson, b. 1 Aug 1776, d. 2 Nov 1843 & Ingeleiv Johannesdatter, b. 13 Mar 1779, d. 4 Sep 1858 – 24 May 1829

Anders Pederson (son):

Residence – Skjerven, Vik – May 24, 1829

Occupation – Bachelor – May 24, 1829

Birth Place – Skjerven, Vik

Ingeleiv Johannesdatter, daughter of Johannes Ambiørnson & Gjertrud Nielsdatter from Kinni, Vik (daughter-in-law):

Birth Place – Kinni, Vik

Berdal, Leikanger

- o Joen Pederson – b. 11 May 1783
- o Endre Pederson – b. 23 Sep 1788, d. 22 Mar 1792

Peder Andersson (father):

Residence – Skjerven, Vik – June 15, 1775

Occupation – Corporal – February 2, 1775

Synneva Joendatter (mother):

Residence – Espesæter, Vik – June 15, 1775

- Peder Endreson & Mette Unknown

  o Anna Pederdatter – b. 30 Jan 1860, chr. 11 Mar 1860

    ### Anna Pederdatter (daughter):

    #### Remarks at Birth – illegitimate

    #### Also Known As – Anna Pederdatter Skjerven

Peder Endreson (father):

Occupation – Bachelor – March 11, 1860

Also Known As – Peder Endreson Skjerven

- Peder Johnson (1st Marriage), b. 6 Sep 1792, d. 22 Nov 1882 & Ingeborg Nielsdatter, b. 11 Oct 1807, d. 14 Oct 1828 – 10 Jan 1828

Peder Johnson, son of John Olsson & Luci Olsdatter from Finden (husband):

Residence – Skjerven – January 10, 1828

Occupation – Bachelor – January 10, 1828

Farmer – January 10, 1828

Birth Place – Finden, Vik

Also Known As – Peder Johnson Finden

Ingeborg Nielsdatter, daughter of Niels Monsson & Anna Siurdatter from Skjerven (wife):

> **Birth Place – Skjerven, Vik**

- Peder Johnson (2nd Marriage), b. 6 Sep 1792 & Synneva Ellingdatter, b. 13 Jan 1790 – 19 Feb 1830
  - John Pederson – b. 29 May 1831, chr. 5 Jun 1831 & Britha Ellingdatter, b. 22 Nov 1832, chr. 25 Nov 1832, d. Mar 6, 1894 – 28 Apr 1860
    - Synneva Johndatter – b. 6 Mar 1861, d. 7 Mar 1861

> **Synneva Johndatter (daughter):**
>
> > **Remarks – born dead**

> **John Pederson (son):**
>
> > **Residence – Skjerven, Vik – April 28, 1860**
> >
> > **Occupation – Bachelor – April 28, 1860**
> >
> > > **Farmer – March 6, 1861**
> >
> > **Christening – Hopperstad Parish**
> >
> > **Birth Place – Skjerven, Vik**
> >
> > **Also Known As – John Pederson Skjerven**

Britha Ellingdatter, daughter of Elling Andersson, b. 25 Oct 1795, d. 18 May 1852, & Britha Olsdatter, b. 29 Jun 1806, d. 19 Oct 1889, married on 15 Jun 1830, from Skjerven (daughter-in-law):

Residence – Skjerven, Vik – April 28, 1860

Christening – Hopperstad Parish

Birth Place – Skjerven, Vik

Also Known As – Britha Ellingdatter Skjerven

o Ingeborg Pederdatter – b. 14 May 1833, chr. 26 May 1833, d. 19 Jul 1853

Ingeborg Pederdatter (daughter):

Christening – Hopperstad Parish

Peder Johnson, son of John Olsson & Luci Olsdatter from Finden (father):

Residence – Skjerven, Vik – February 19, 1830

Occupation – Farmer – June 5, 1831

May 26, 1833

Relationship Status – widower – February 19, 1830

Birth Place – Finden, Vik

Synneva Ellingdatter, daughter of Elling Joenson & Anna Erikdatter from Holstad (mother):

Birth Place – Holstad, Vik

- Peder Olsson, b. 23 Dec 1863, chr. 17 Jan 1864, & Martha Olsdatter, b. 30 May 1868, chr. 2 Aug 1868 – 16 Feb 1893

  o Anna Mari Pederdatter – b. 14 Mar 1893, chr. 2 Apr 1893

Peder Olsson, son of Ole Pederson & Martha Ingebrigtdatter from Vikøyri (father):

Residence – Skjerven, Vik – February 16, 1893

Occupation – Laborer, Worker – February 16, 1893

April 2, 1893

Birth Place – Vikøren, Vik

Also Known As – Peder Olsson Skjerven

Martha Olsdatter, daughter of Ole Olsson & Anna Ellingdatter from Bø (mother):

Birth Place – Bø, Vik

- Peder Olsson, b. 1792, d. 1 Jan 1838 & Torbjørg Anfinddatter, b. 1781, d. 18 Aug 1845 – 2 Jan 1827

  o Anna Pederdatter – b. 15 Sep 1825, chr. 18 Sep 1825

  ### Anna Pederdatter (daughter):

  Christening – Hopperstad Parish

  Also Known As – Anna Pederdatter Skjerven

  o Martha Pederdatter – b. 3 Feb 1829, chr. 8 Feb 1829

  ### Martha Pederdatter (daughter):

  Christening – Hopperstad Parish

Peder Olsson (father):

Residence – Midlang – September 18, 1825

  Skjerven, Vik – January 2, 1827

Occupation – Bachelor – September 18, 1825

  January 2, 1827

  Militia – September 18, 1825

  January 2, 1827

  Smallholder, Cottager – February 8, 1829

Birth Place – Skjerven, Vik

Torbjørg Anfinddatter (mother):

Birth Place – Midlang, Vik

- Roland Pederson & Britha Larsdatter

  o Gjertrud Rolanddatter – b. 23 Feb 1803, d. 8 Mar 1803

  ### Gjertrud Rolanddatter (daughter):

  ### Age at Death – 14 days

- Siur Iverson, b. 1739, d. 22 Feb 1778 & Britha Olsdatter – 20 Jan 1764

  o Mikkel Siurson, b. 12 Dec 1762 & Synneva Thomasdatter, b. 1768, d. 14 May 1838 – 4 Jun 1791

  ▪ Anna Mikkeldatter – b. 6 Jul 1792

  ▪ Britha Mikkeldatter – b. 15 Jun 1795

    ### Britha Mikkeldatter (daughter):

    ### Remarks about Birth – mother listed as
    ### Synneva Hermunddatter

  ▪ Siur Mikkelson – b. 5 Jan 1800, d. 2 Mar 1824

    ### Siur Mikkelson (son):

    ### Remarks about Birth – twin to Thomas Mikkelson

- Thomas Mikkelson, b. 5 Jan 1800 & Britha Hermunddatter, b. 21 Jan 1802 – 9 Oct 1831

  - Inger Thomasdatter – b. 4 Mar 1829, chr. 5 Apr 1829 & Peder Johannesson, b. 1834 – 2 Jan 1859

    - Johannes Pederson – b. 15 Sep 1856, chr. 12 Oct 1856

      ### Johannes Pederson (son):

      Christening – Hopperstad Church

      Remarks about Birth – illegitimate

      Also Known As – Johannes Pederson Skjerven

    - Hermund Pederson – b. 9 Oct 1859, chr. 23 Oct 1859

    - Britha Pederdatter – b. 24 Dec 1862, chr. 8 Feb 1863

    ### Inger Thomsdatter (daughter):

    Residence – Skjerven, Vik – January 2, 1859

    Christening – Hopperstad Parish

    Remarks about Birth – illegitimate

    Birth Place – Skjerven, Vik

    Also Known As – Inger Thomasdatter Skjerven

Skjerven Gaard Vik Sogn og Fjordane Norway: 1669 to 1922

Peder Johannnesson (son-in-law):

Residence – Skjerven, Vik – October 12, 1856

Føli, Vik – January 2, 1859

October 23, 1859

February 8, 1863

Occupation – Bachelor – October 12, 1856

January 2, 1859

Smallholder, Cottager – October 23, 1859

Farmer – February 8, 1863

Birth Place – Føli, Vik

Also Known As – Peder Johannesson Føli

- Synneva Thomasdatter – b. 23 Oct 1831, chr. 13 Nov 1831

Synneva Thomasdatter (daughter):

Christening – Hopperstad Parish

- Siur Thomasson – b. 24 Sep 1834, chr. 5 Oct 1834

Siur Thomasson (son):

Christening – Hopperstad Parish

- Alis Thomasdatter – b. 27 Apr 1838, chr. 13 May 1838, d. 2 Sep 1838

  ## Alis Thomasdatter (daughter):

  ### Christening – **Hopperstad Parish**

- Hermund Thomasson – b. 19 Dec 1839, chr. 25 Dec 1839, d. 28 Nov 1844

  ## Hermund Thomasson (son):

  ### Christening – **Hopperstad Parish**

- Ole Thomasson – b. 12 Feb 1843

Thomas Mikkelson (son):

Residence – **Fjærestad, Vik – April 5, 1829**

Skjerven, Vik – October 9, 1831

Hopperstad – October 5, 1834

May 13, 1838

Occupation – **Bachelor – April 5, 1829**

October 9, 1831

Soldier – October 9, 1831

Renter – November 13, 1831

Farmer – October 5, 1834

Smallholder, Cottager – May 13, 1838

December 19, 1839

February 12, 1843

Birth Place – Skjerven, Vik

Also Known As – Thomas Mikkelson Skjerven

Britha Hermunddatter, daughter of Hermund Ingebrigtson & Alis Hermunddatter from Skjerven (daughter-in-law):

Birth Place – Fjærestad, Vik

Mikkel Siurson (son of Siur Iverson & Britha Olsdatter):

Residence – Skjerven, Vik – June 4, 1791

Brejen, Vik – July 6, 1792

June 15, 1795

January 5, 1800

Strand, Vik – January 5, 1800

Remarks about Birth – illegitimate

Synneva Thomasdatter (daughter-in-law):

Residence – Midlang, Vik – June 4, 1791

- Botilda Siurdatter – b. 30 Jan 1765

- Iver Siurson – b. 28 September 1769

- Ole Siurson – b. 3 Mar 1772

Ole Siurson (son):

Remarks – born March 3rd

Remarks about Birth – twin to Kari Siurdatter

- Kari Siurdatter – b. 3 Mar 1772

Kari Siurdatter (daughter):

Remarks – born March 2nd

Remarks about birth – twin to Ole Siurson

Siur Iverson (father):

Residence – Holstad, Vik – January 20, 1764

Occupation – Soldier

Remarks – From Holstad

Remarks about Marriage – they have a child together

Birth Place – Vik

Britha Olsdatter (mother):

Residence – Skjerven, Vik – January 20, 1764

Birth Place – Vik

- Thor Bendixson & Synneva Andersdatter – 6 Jan 1779

  o Ragnhild Thorsdatter – b. 3 Nov 1778

  o Kari Thordatter – b. 6 Jan 1781

  ### Kari Thordatter (daughter):

  #### Christening – Vik Parish

  o Synneva Thordatter – b. 15 Mar 1790

  o Helga Thordatter – b. 4 Apr 1793

  o Luci Thordatter – b. 9 Jun 1796

Thor Bendixson (father):

Residence – Skjerven, Vik – November 3, 1778

Rosheim, Vik – January 6, 1779

Holstad, Vik – March 15, 1790

April 4, 1793

June 9, 1796

Occupation – Soldier – January 6, 1779

Synneva Andersdatter (mother):

Residence – Skjerven, Vik – January 6, 1779

Individual Births/Baptisms

None were listed

Individual Burials

- Anders Ellingson – b. 1829, d. 3 Sep 1903

Anders Ellingson (deceased):

Cause of Death – abdomen disease

- Anders Siurson – b. 1711, d. 19 Jun 1740

Anders Siurson (deceased):

Occupation – Soldier – Before June 19, 1740

- Anna Ellingdatter – b. 1824, d. 11 Apr 1905

Anna Ellingdatter (deceased):

Cause of Death – old age, weakness

Also Known As – Anna Ellingdatter Bø

- Anna Olsdatter – b. 1807, d. 5 Mar 1892

Anna Olsdatter (deceased):

Also Known As – Anna Olsdatter Bø

- Anna Pederdatter – b. 1732, d. 23 Dec 1808

- Anna Siurdatter – b. 1771, d. 25 Oct 1826

- Botolph Endreson – b. 1726, d. 6 Jan 1758

- Botolph Ingebrigtson – b. 1774, d. 24 Jul 1852

- Botolph Pederson – b. 1785, d. 25 Apr 1828

- Botilda Mikkeldatter – b. 1713, d. 1 Jul 1764, bur. 31 Mar 1764

Botilda Mikkeldatter (deceased):

Remarks about Burial – her husband's interment was the same day

- Britha Botholphdatter – b. 1810, d. 6 Oct 1868

- Britha Hermunddatter – b. 1660, d. 31 May 1744

Britha Hermunddatter (deceased):

Remark about Death – gentlewoman

Age at Death – 84 years, 7 weeks

- Britha Hermunddatter – b. 1737, d. 8 Nov 1817

- Britha Johndatter – b. 1793, d. 30 Nov 1845

- Britha Olsdatter – b. 1738, d. 28 Jun 1821

- Endre Botolphson – b. 1693, d. 4 Mar 1759

Endre Botholphson (deceased):

Age at Death – 65 ½ years and some weeks

- Endre Hermundson – b. 1721, d. 29 Jun 1791

- Endre Olsson – b. 1723, d. 7 Apr 1790

- Gietlau Larsdatter – b. 1776, d. 19 May 1850

- Guthorm Ingebrigtson – b. 1835, d. 30 May 1846

- Hans Nielsson – b. 1750, d. 22 Nov 1750

Hans Nielsson (deceased):

Remarks about Birth – illegitimate child

Age at Death – 16 weeks

- Helga Olsdatter – b. 1671, d. 14 May 1752

Helga Olsdatter (deceased):

Remarks about Death – gentlewoman

- Ingebrigt Pederson – b. 1734, d. 2 Jan 1822

- Iver Heljeson – b. 1797, d. 24 Feb 1882

Iver Heljeson (deceased):

Also Known As – Iver Heljeson Ovrid

- Joen Andersson – b. 1674, d. 25 Jan 1739

- Joen Markusson – b. 1659, d. 25 Mar 1733

- Johannes Lasseson – b. 1703, d. 4 Mar 1759

Johannes Lasseson (deceased):

Age at Death – 55 years, 18 weeks

- Kari Endredatter – b. 1719, d. 17 Nov 1807

- Magne Endreson – b. 1846, d. 23 Jan 1846

- Martha Larsdatter – b. 1665, d. 11 Sep 1746

Martha Larsdatter (deceased):

Remarks about Death – gentlewoman from Tryti

- Martha Pederdatter – b. 1691, d. 11 Dec 1774

Martha Pederdatter (deceased):

Age at Death – 83 ½ years

Cause of Death – old age

- Martha Pederdatter – b. 1820, d. 11 Jul 1829

- Mikkel Olsson – b. 1737, d. 7 Feb 1762

Mikkel Olsson (deceased):

Age at Death – 24 ½ years

Cause of Death – drowned in the ice on the road to Voss

- Niels Hansson – b. 1770, d. 21 Apr 1850

- Ole Iverson – b. 1833, d. 1 Feb 1856

- Ole Iverson – b. 1823, d. 29 Oct 1906

Ole Iverson (deceased):

Cause of Death – heart paralysis

Also Known As – Ole Iverson Midlang

- Ole Joenson – b. 1686, d. 29 Sep 1758

- Ole Kolbeinson – b. 1714, d. 1 Jul 1764, bur. 27 Apr 1764

Ole Kolbeinson (deceased):

Remarks about Burial – his wife's interment was the same day

- Olina Hansdatter – b. 1840, d. 19 Feb 1863

- Peder Rolandson – b. 1834, d. 23 Dec 1864

- Ragnhild Andersdatter – b. 1727, d. 14 Feb 1826

- Randi Ellingdatter – b. 1735, d. 10 Dec 1741

Randi Ellingdatter (deceased):

Cause of death – smallpox

Age at Death – 6 ½ years, 8 days

- Randi Ellingdatter – b. 1762, d. 9 Apr 1820

- Randi Hansdatter – b. 1712, d. 17 Nov 1782

- Siur Andersson – b. 1669, d. 4 Jun 1747

Siur Andersson (deceased):

Remarks about Death – gentleman

- Synneva Andersdatter – b. 1790, d. 3 Feb 1860

- Synneva Ellingdatter – b. 1751, d. 8 Aug 1800

- Synneva Joendatter – b. 1702, d. 2 Apr 1775

Synneva Joendatter (deceased):

Cause of Death – old age

- Synneva Johndatter – b. 1750, d. 23 Jun 1824

- Unni Nielsdatter – b. 1713, d. Jul 1783

Individual Marriages

- Anna Andersdatter & Johannes Olsson – 10 Nov 1743

Anna Andersdatter (wife):

Residence – Skjerven, Vik – November 10, 1743

Remarks about Marriage – bride pregnant

Johannes Olsson (husband):

Residence – Djuvvik, Vik – November 10, 1743

Relationship Status at Marriage – widow

- Anna Endredatter & Joen Guthormson – 10 Jul 1749

Anna Endredatter (wife):

Residence – Skjerven, Vik – July 10, 1749

Joen Guthormson (husband):

Residence – Espesæter, Vik – July 10, 1749

- Anna Olsdatter, b. 1827 & Johannes Anfindson, b. 1829 – 24 Jun 1856

  o Gjertrud Johannesdatter – b. 14 Feb 1850, chr. 22 Feb 1850

Gjertrud Johannesdatter (daughter):

Christening – Hove Church

Remarks about Birth – illegitimate

o Anna Johannesdatter – b. 3 Jan 1858, chr. 7 Feb 1858

Anna Olsdatter (wife):

Residence – Skjerven, Vik – June 24, 1856

Birth Place – Skjerven, Vik

Also Known As – Anna Olsdatter Skjerven

Johannes Anfindson (husband):

Residence – Vikøyri, Vik – February 22, 1850

Grov, Vik – June 24, 1856

Occupation – Bachelor – February 22, 1850

June 24, 1856

Birth Place – Voll, Vik

Also Known As – Johannes Anfindson Voll

- Britha Andersdatter & Knud Botholphson – 30 Jun 1737

Britha Andersdatter (wife):

Residence – Skjerven, Vik – June 30, 1737

Remarks about Marriage – bride pregnant

Knud Botholphson (husband):

Residence – Vik almenning, Vik – June 30, 1737

Remarks about Marriage – bridegroom from Vikøyri

Relationship Status at Marriage – widow

- Britha Ellingdatter & Lars Andersson – 28 Dec 1778

Britha Ellingdatter (wife):

Residence – Skjerven, Vik – December 28, 1778

Lars Andersson (husband):

Residence – Seim, Vik – December 28, 1778

Occupation – Soldier – December 28, 1778

Remarks about Marriage – bridegroom from Seimsøyri

Engagement – Vetløyri

- Britha Olsdatter (2nd Marriage) & Ole Knudson – 28 Dec 1779

Britha Olsdatter (wife):

Residence – Skjerven, Vik – December 28, 1779

Ole Knudson (husband):

Residence – Seim, Vik – December 28, 1779

Remarks about Marriage – bridegroom from Seimsøyri

- Gietlau Joendatter, b. 1707, d. 23 Oct 1781 & Elling Guthormson, b. 1704, d. 5 Feb 1775 – 2 Jul 1733

Gietlau Joendatter (wife):

Residence – Skjerven, Vik – July 2, 1733

Remarks about Marriage – bride pregnant

Royal letter (needed to get married)

cousins

Elling Guthormson (husband):

Residence – Hønsi, Vik – July 2, 1733

Occupation – Soldier – July 2, 1733

Age at Death – 70 ½ years

Cause of Death – old age

- Gjøri Ellenddatter, b. 11 Dec 1865, chr. 25 Feb 1866 & Johannes Endreson, b. 15 Jan 1867, chr. 3 Mar 1867 – 1 Jun 1904

Gjøri Ellenddatter, daughter of Ellend Johnson & Synneva Ellingdatter from Holstad (wife):

Residence – Skjerven, Vik – June 1, 1904

Birth Place – Holstad, Vik

Also Known As – Gjøri Ellenddatter Holstad

Johannes Endreson, son of Endre Bendixson & Anna Johannesdatter from Holstad (husband):

Residence – Holstad, Vik – June 1, 1904

Occupation – Farmer – June 1, 1904

Birth Place – Holstad, Vik

Also Known As – Johannes Endreson Holstad

- Ingeborg Aamunddatter & Herumnd Tollakson – 23 Jun 1769

Ingeborg Aamunddatter (wife):

Residence – Skjerven, Vik – June 23, 1769

Birth Place – Vik

Hermund Tollakson (husband):

Residence – Undi, Vik – June 23, 1769

Occupation – Soldier – June 23, 1769

Birth Place – Vik

- Kari Endredatter & Anders Joenson – 6 Jan 1745

Kari Endredatter (wife):

Residence – Skjerven, Vik – January 6, 1745

Anders Joenson (husband):

Residence – Tenål, Vik – January 6, 1745

Occupation – Militia – January 6, 1745

- Kari Siurdatter & Christen Christenson – 30 May 1804

Kari Siurdatter (wife):

Residence – Skjerven, Vik – May 30, 1804

Christen Christenson (husband):

Residence – Tryti, Vik – May 30, 1804

Occupation – Soldier – May 30, 1804

- Luci Endredatter & Endre Erikson – 6 Apr 1790

Luci Endredatter (wife):

Residence – Skjerven, Vik – April 6, 1790

Endre Erikson (husband):

Residence – Tryti, Vik – April 6, 1790

Occupation – Corporal – April 6, 1790

- Magnild Joendatter & Tollaf Hermundson – 6 Jan 1737

Magnild Joendatter (wife):

Residence – Skjerven, Vik – January 6, 1737

Tollaf Hermundson (husband):

Residence – Undi, Vik – January 6, 1737

Relationship Status at Marriage – widow

- Martha Joendatter, b. 1688, d. 19 Jul 1767 & Palme Hellieson – 6 Jan 1731

Martha Joendatter (wife):

> **Residence** – Skjerven, Vik – January 6, 1731

> **Remarks at Burial** – gentlewoman

Palme Hellieson (husband):

> **Residence** – Bø, Vik – January 6, 1731

- Ragnhild Olsdatter & Joen Arneson – 30 Nov 1732

Ragnhild Olsdatter (wife):

> **Residence** – Skjerven, Vik – November 30, 1732

> **Remarks about Marriage** – bride pregnant

> Seimsøyri

Joen Arneson (husband):

> **Residence** – Seim, Vik – November 30, 1732

- Randi Endredatter & Erik Ellendson – 15 Feb 1753

Randi Endredatter (wife):

Residence – Skjerven, Vik – February 15, 1753

Remarks about Marriage – bride pregnant

Erik Ellendson (husband):

Residence – Tryti, Vik – February 15, 1753

Occupation – Soldier – February 15, 1753

Remarks about Marriage – married in Hopperstad Church

- Randi Endredatter & Ole Olsson – 31 May 1774

Randi Endredatter (wife):

Residence – Skjerven, Vik – May 31, 1774

Ole Olsson (husband):

Residence – Stadheim, Vik – May 31, 1774

- Sigrid Endredatter & Guthorm Anfindson – 10 Jan 1758

Sigrid Endredatter (wife):

Residence – Skjerven, Vik – January 10, 1758

Guthorm Anfindson (husband):

Residence – Midlang, Vik – January 10, 1758

Remarks about Marriage – married in Hopperstad Church

Name Variations

People

Aamund = Åmund

Albrigt = Albricht, Albrict, Albrect

Ambiørn = Ambjørn

Anfind = Andfind, Andfinn, Anfinn

Anna = Anne

Axel = Aksel

Bendix = Bendiks

Bohilda = Bohilde

Botholph = Botolph Bottolv, Buttolv, Botolf, Bottolf, Bottol, Butolf

Britha = Brithe, Brite

Dordei = Durdei

Elsa = Else

Eli = Elie, Ely

Erik = Eric, Erich

Gietlau = Gitlau, Gitlaug, Gitloug, Gitløv

Gjertrud = Giertrud, Gertrud

Gjøri = Gjørri, Giørri

Guthorm = Gutorm, Guttorm

Halvor = Halvar, Haldor

Helje = Helge

Ingeborg = Ingebor

Ingebrigt = Ingebright, Ingebricht, Ingebrict

Ingeleiv = Ingelev

Inger = Inga

Ingerid = Ingrid

Iver = Ivar

Joen = Jon, John

Johannes = Johannis

Kari = Karie

Kolbein = Colbein, Colben

Kristi = Kristie, Christi, Christie

Luci = Lucie, Lussi, Lussie

Magnild = Magnilde

Mari = Marie

Markus = Marcus

Martha = Martha, Marthe, Marta, Marita, Maritha,

Margretha, Margrethe

Mette = Methe

Mikkel = Michel

Olina = Oline

Palme = Palne

Peder = Per, Peer

Ragnhild = Ragnhilde, Ragnilla

Sigrid = Siri, Sigrud

Sigtona = Sigtone

Siur = Sjur

Synneva = Sønneve, Synneve

Thor = Tor

Tollaf = Tollav, Tollag

Tollak = Tollach

Vasson = Wasson

Vilhelm = Wilhelm

Places

Bø = Bøe

Brejen = Breijen

Dahle = Dale

Fjærestad = Fierestad

Føli = Følie, Følid

Hønsi = Hønsie

Orvedal = Aarvedal, Årvedal

Sæbø = Sæbøe

Skjerven = Skierven, Scherven, Schierven

Stokkebø = Stokkebøe

Tenål = Tenaal

Tryti = Trytten, Trytti, Tryttie

Vangsnes = Wangsnes

Vigøren = Wigøren, Wiigøren, Vikøren

Notes

Notes

Notes

Notes

Notes

Note

Index

A

B

C

E

F

G

ħ

Hurst

m

N

O

Skjerven Gaard Vik Sogn og Fjordane Norway: 1669 to 1922

About The Author

Donovan Hurst graduated from San Diego State University with a Bachelor of Arts in the major field of studies of History and a minor in the field of studies of Anthropology. He is a current member of The General Society of Mayflower Descendants and has been conducting genealogical research for over 10 years tracing back his ancestors to their ancestral homelands in Denmark, England, France, Germany, Ireland, Norway, and Scotland.

www.ingramcontent.com/pod-product-compliance
Lightning Source LLC
Chambersburg PA
CBHW081154270326
41930CB00014B/3150